contents

2-step skillet chicken broccoli divan

prep 10 minutes I **cook** 15 minutes I **makes** 4 servings

- 1 **tablespoon butter**
- 4 **skinless, boneless chicken breast halves (about 1 pound), cut into 1-inch pieces**
- 3 **cups fresh *or* frozen broccoli florets**
- 1 **can (10¾ ounces) Campbell's® Condensed Cream of Chicken Soup (Regular *or* 98% Fat Free)**
- ½ **cup milk**
- ½ **cup shredded Cheddar cheese**

1. Heat the butter in a 10-inch skillet over medium-high heat. Add the chicken and cook until well browned, stirring often.

2. Stir the broccoli, soup and milk in the skillet. Reduce the heat to low. Cover and cook for 5 minutes or until the chicken is cooked through. Sprinkle with the cheese.

tip *Try this recipe with Campbell's® Cream of Mushroom Soup **and** shredded Swiss cheese.*

beef & pasta

prep 5 minutes | **cook** 25 minutes | **makes** 4 servings

- ¾ **pound ground beef (85% lean)**
- 1¾ **cups Swanson® Vegetable Broth (Regular *or* Certified Organic)**
- 1 **tablespoon Worcestershire sauce**
- ½ **teaspoon dried oregano leaves, crushed**
- ½ **teaspoon garlic powder**
- 1 **can (about 8 ounces) stewed tomatoes**
- 1½ **cups *uncooked* medium tube-shaped (ziti) *or* corkscrew-shaped (rotini) pasta**

1. Cook the beef in a 10-inch skillet over medium-high heat until it's well browned, stirring often to separate the meat. Pour off any fat.

2. Stir the broth, Worcestershire, oregano, garlic powder and tomatoes in the skillet and heat to a boil. Stir in the pasta. Reduce the heat to low. Cover and cook for 10 minutes, stirring often. **Uncover**.

3. Cook for 5 minutes or until the pasta is tender.

tuna & pasta cheddar melt

prep 10 minutes | **cook** 15 minutes | **makes** 4 servings

- 1 can (10½ ounces) Campbell's® Condensed Chicken Broth
- 1 soup can water
- 3 cups *uncooked* corkscrew-shaped pasta (rotini)
- 1 can (10¾ ounces) Campbell's® Condensed Cream of Mushroom Soup (Regular *or* 98% Fat Free)
- 1 cup milk
- 1 can (about 6 ounces) tuna, drained and flaked
- 1 cup shredded Cheddar cheese (about 4 ounces)
- 2 tablespoons Italian-seasoned dry bread crumbs
- 2 teaspoons butter, melted

1. Heat the broth and water in a 12-inch skillet over medium-high heat to a boil. Stir in the pasta. Reduce the heat to medium. Cook until the pasta is tender, stirring often. Do not drain.

2. Stir the soup, milk and tuna in the skillet. Top with the cheese. Stir the bread crumbs and butter in a small bowl. Sprinkle over the tuna mixture. Cook until the cheese is melted.

20-minute turkey & rice

prep 10 minutes | **cook** 10 minutes | **makes** 4 servings

- 1 can (10¾ ounces) Campbell's® Condensed Cream of Chicken Soup (Regular *or* 98% Fat Free)
- 1½ cups water
- ¼ teaspoon paprika
- ¼ teaspoon ground black pepper
- 2 cups *uncooked* instant white rice
- 2 cups cubed cooked turkey
- 2 cups cooked vegetable combination (carrots, green beans, peas)

Heat the soup, water, paprika and black pepper in a 10-inch skillet over medium-high heat to a boil. Stir in the rice, turkey and vegetables. Reduce the heat to low. Cook for 5 minutes or until the rice is tender.

beef taco skillet

prep 5 minutes I **cook** 20 minutes I **makes** 4 servings

- 1 pound ground beef
- 1 can (10¾ ounces) Campbell's® Condensed Tomato Soup (Regular **or** Healthy Request®)
- ½ cup Pace® Picante Sauce
- ½ cup water
- 6 flour tortillas (6-inch), cut into 1-inch pieces
- ½ cup shredded Cheddar cheese

1. Cook the beef in a 10-inch skillet over medium-high heat until well browned, stirring often to separate the meat. Pour off any fat.

2. Stir the soup, picante sauce, water and tortillas in the skillet and heat to a boil. Reduce the heat to low. Cook for 5 minutes. Stir the beef mixture. Top with the cheese.

Creamy Mexican Fiesta: Stir in ½ *cup* sour cream with the soup.

Ranchero Style: Use corn tortillas instead of flour tortillas and shredded Mexican cheese blend instead of Cheddar.

fish & vegetable skillet

prep 15 minutes | **cook** 15 minutes | **makes** 4 servings

¼ cup water

2 tablespoons dry white wine (optional)

½ teaspoon dried thyme leaves, crushed

Generous dash ground black pepper

1 large carrot, cut into matchstick-thin strips (about 1 cup)

2 stalks celery, cut into matchstick-thin strips (about 1⅓ cups)

1 small onion, chopped (about ¼ cup)

1 can (10¾ ounces) Campbell's® Condensed Cream of Mushroom Soup (Regular, 98% Fat Free *or* Healthy Request®)

4 firm white fish fillets (cod, haddock *or* halibut) (about 1 pound)

1. Heat the water, wine, thyme, black pepper, carrot, celery and onion in a 10-inch skillet over medium-high heat to a boil. Reduce the heat to low. Cover and cook for 5 minutes or until the vegetables are tender-crisp.

2. Stir the soup in the skillet. Top with the fish. Cover and cook for 5 minutes or until the fish flakes easily when tested with a fork.

quick & easy dinner nachos supreme

prep 10 minutes I **cook** 15 minutes I **makes** 4 servings

- 1 **pound ground beef**
- 1 **package (about 1 ounce) taco seasoning mix**
- 1 **can (10¾ ounces) Campbell's® Condensed Tomato Soup**
- 1½ **cups water**
- 1½ **cups *uncooked* instant white rice**
    Pace® Chunky Salsa
    Shredded Cheddar cheese
    Shredded lettuce
    Tortilla chips

1. Cook the beef and taco seasoning in a 10-inch skillet until the beef is well browned, stirring often to separate the meat. Pour off any fat.

2. Stir the soup, water and rice in the skillet and heat to a boil. Reduce the heat to low. Cover and cook for 5 minutes or until the rice is tender.

3. Top with the salsa, cheese and lettuce. Serve with the tortilla chips for dipping.

skillet pork chops florentine

prep 5 minutes | **cook** 30 minutes | **makes** 6 servings

- 2 tablespoons olive **or** vegetable oil
- 6 boneless pork chops, ¾-inch thick (about 1½ pounds)
- 1 medium onion, thinly sliced (about ½ cup)
- 1 jar (24 ounces) Prego® Marinara Italian Sauce
- 1 package (10 ounces) frozen leaf spinach, thawed and well drained
- 4 ounces shredded mozzarella cheese (about 1 cup)

1. Heat **1 tablespoon** of the oil in a 12-inch skillet over medium-high heat. Add the pork chops and cook until the chops are well browned on both sides. Remove the pork chops and set them aside.

2. Reduce the heat to medium and add the remaining oil. Add the onion. Cook and stir until the onion is tender-crisp.

3. Stir the Italian sauce and spinach into the skillet and heat to a boil. Return the pork chops to the skillet and reduce the heat to low. Cover and cook until the chops are cooked through. Sprinkle with the cheese.

tip *To thaw spinach, microwave on HIGH for 3 minutes, breaking apart with a fork halfway through heating.*

quick chicken parmesan

prep 5 minutes I **bake** 25 minutes I **makes** 4 servings

- 4 skinless, boneless chicken breast halves (about 1 pound)
- 2 cups Prego® Traditional Italian Sauce *or* Fresh Mushroom Italian Sauce
- 2 ounces shredded mozzarella cheese (about ½ cup)
- 2 tablespoons grated Parmesan cheese
- ½ of a 16-ounce package spaghetti, cooked and drained (about 4 cups)

1. Place the chicken in a 2-quart shallow baking dish. Top the chicken with the Italian sauce. Sprinkle with the mozzarella cheese and Parmesan cheese.

2. Bake at 400°F. for 25 minutes or until cooked through. Serve with the spaghetti.

pork with mushroom dijon sauce

prep 10 minutes | **cook** 30 minutes | **makes** 4 servings

- 4 boneless pork chops, ¾-inch thick (about 1 pound)
- ½ teaspoon lemon pepper seasoning
- 1 tablespoon vegetable oil
- 1 cup sliced mushrooms (about 3 ounces)
- 1 can (10¾ ounces) Campbell's® Condensed Cream of Mushroom Soup (Regular *or* 98% Fat Free)
- ¼ cup milk
- 2 tablespoons Chablis *or* other dry white wine
- 1 tablespoon Dijon-style mustard

1. Season the pork with the lemon pepper.

2. Heat the oil in a 10-inch skillet over medium-high heat. Add the pork and cook until it's well browned on both sides. Remove the pork from the skillet.

3. Add the mushrooms to the skillet. Reduce the heat to medium. Cook until the mushrooms are tender, stirring occasionally.

4. Stir the soup, milk, wine and mustard in the skillet and heat to a boil. Return the pork to the skillet. Reduce the heat to low. Cover and cook for 10 minutes or until the pork is cooked through.

one-dish beef stroganoff

prep 15 minutes I **cook** 20 minutes I **makes** 4 servings

   1 **tablespoon vegetable oil**
   1 **boneless beef sirloin steak, ¾-inch thick (about 1 pound),**
      cut into thin strips
   1 **medium onion, chopped (about ½ cup)**
   3 **cloves garlic, minced**
   1 **teaspoon dried parsley flakes**
1¾ **cups Swanson® Beef Stock**
   2 **cups sliced mushrooms (about 6 ounces)**
   3 **cups _uncooked_ medium egg noodles**
  ½ **cup sour cream**
    Chopped fresh parsley

1. Heat the oil in a 12-inch nonstick skillet over medium-high heat. Add the beef and cook until it's well browned, stirring often. Add the onion, garlic and parsley and cook until the onion is tender-crisp.

2. Stir the stock and mushrooms in the skillet and heat to a boil. Stir in the noodles. Reduce the heat to low. Cover and cook for 10 minutes or until the noodles are tender.

3. Stir the sour cream in the skillet and cook until the mixture is hot and bubbling. Sprinkle with the parsley.

shortcut chicken cordon bleu

prep 10 minutes I **cook** 20 minutes I **makes** 4 servings

- 1 tablespoon butter
- 4 skinless, boneless chicken breast halves (about 1 pound)
- 1 can (10¾ ounces) Campbell's® Condensed Cream of Chicken Soup (Regular *or* 98% Fat Free)
- 2 tablespoons water
- 2 tablespoons Chablis *or* other dry white wine
- ½ cup shredded Swiss cheese
- ½ cup chopped cooked ham
- 4 cups medium egg noodles, cooked and drained

1. Heat the butter in a 10-inch skillet over medium–high heat. Add the chicken and cook for 10 minutes or until well browned on both sides.

2. Stir the soup, water, wine, cheese and ham in the skillet and heat to a boil. Reduce the heat to low. Cover and cook for 5 minutes or until the chicken is cooked through. Serve the chicken and sauce with the noodles.

easy asian-style chicken & rice

prep 5 minutes I **cook** 20 minutes I **makes** 4 servings

- 1 tablespoon vegetable oil
- 4 skinless, boneless chicken breast halves (about 1 pound)
- 1 can (10¾ ounces) Campbell's® Condensed Golden Mushroom Soup
- 1½ cups water
- 1 package (1.25 ounces) teriyaki seasoning mix
- 1 bag (16 ounces) frozen stir-fry vegetables
- 1½ cups *uncooked* instant white rice

1. Heat the oil in a 10-inch skillet over medium-high heat. Add the chicken and cook until well browned on both sides. Remove the chicken from the skillet.

2. Stir the soup, water, seasoning mix and vegetables in the skillet and heat to a boil. Stir in the rice. Return the chicken to the skillet. Reduce the heat to low. Cover and cook for 5 minutes or until the chicken is cooked through and the rice is tender.

quick skillet ziti

prep 5 minutes | **cook** 20 minutes | **makes** 4 servings

1 **pound ground beef**
1 **jar (24 ounces) Prego® Traditional Italian Sauce or**
   Marinara Italian Sauce
5 **cups tube-shaped pasta (ziti), cooked and drained**
   Grated Parmesan cheese

1. Cook the beef in a 10-inch skillet until it's well browned, stirring often to separate the meat. Pour off any fat.

2. Stir the Italian sauce and pasta in the skillet and heat through. Sprinkle with the cheese.

chicken seasoned rice and vegetable casserole

prep 5 minutes | **bake** 1 hour | **makes** 6 servings

- 1 can (10¾ ounces) Campbell's® Condensed Cream of Mushroom Soup (Regular **or** 98% Fat Free)
- 1 cup water
- 1 package (6 ounces) seasoned long-grain and wild rice mix
- 1 bag (16 ounces) frozen vegetable combination (broccoli, carrots, water chestnuts)
- 1 cup shredded Cheddar cheese (about 4 ounces)
- 6 skinless, boneless chicken breast halves (about 1½ pounds)
  Paprika

1. Stir the soup, water, rice and seasoning packet, vegetables and **half** of the cheese in a 3-quart shallow baking dish. Top with the chicken. Sprinkle the chicken with the paprika. Cover the baking dish.

2. Bake at 375°F. for 1 hour or until the chicken is cooked through and the rice is tender. Uncover the dish and sprinkle with the remaining cheese.

beef & broccoli

prep 10 minutes I **cook** 20 minutes I **makes** 4 servings

1 tablespoon vegetable oil

1 pound boneless beef sirloin steak **or** beef top round steak, ¾-inch thick, cut into thin strips

1 can (10¾ ounces) Campbell's® Condensed Tomato Soup

3 tablespoons soy sauce

1 tablespoon vinegar

1 teaspoon garlic powder

¼ teaspoon crushed red pepper (optional)

3 cups fresh **or** thawed frozen broccoli florets

4 cups hot cooked rice

1. Heat the oil in a 10-inch skillet over medium-high heat. Add the beef and stir-fry until well browned.

2. Stir the soup, soy sauce, vinegar, garlic powder and red pepper, if desired, in the skillet and heat to a boil. Stir in the broccoli and cook until it's tender-crisp. Serve the beef mixture over the rice.

tip *To make slicing easier, freeze the beef for 1 hour.*

3-cheese pasta bake

prep 20 minutes I **bake** 20 minutes I **makes** 4 servings

- 1 can (10¾ ounces) Campbell's® Condensed Cream of Mushroom Soup (Regular *or* 98% Fat Free)
- 1 package (8 ounces) shredded two-cheese blend (about 2 cups)
- ⅓ cup grated Parmesan cheese
- 1 cup milk
- ¼ teaspoon ground black pepper
- 3 cups corkscrew-shaped pasta (rotini), cooked and drained

1. Stir the soup, cheeses, milk and black pepper in a 1½-quart casserole. Stir in the pasta.

2. Bake at 400°F. for 20 minutes or until the mixture is hot and bubbling.

tip *Substitute 2 cups of your favorite shredded cheese for the two-cheese blend.*

cheddar penne with sausage & peppers

prep 20 minutes | **cook** 20 minutes | **makes** 6 servings

1 tablespoon olive oil

1 pound sweet Italian pork sausage, cut into ½-inch slices

1 large green pepper, cut into 2-inch-long strips (about 2 cups)

1 large onion, sliced (about 1 cup)

3 cloves garlic, minced

1 can (10¾ ounces) Campbell's® Condensed Cheddar Cheese Soup

½ cup milk

2 cups penne pasta, cooked and drained

1. Heat the oil in a 10-inch skillet over medium-high heat. Add the sausage and cook until well browned, stirring occasionally. Remove the sausage from the skillet. Pour off any fat.

2. Add the pepper and onion to the skillet and cook until the vegetables are tender, stirring occasionally. Add the garlic and cook and stir for 1 minute. Stir in the soup and milk and heat to a boil. Return the sausage to the skillet. Reduce the heat to low. Cook until the sausage is cooked through, stirring occasionally.

3. Place the pasta into a large bowl. Add the sausage mixture and toss to coat.

tip *You may substitute hot Italian sausage for the sweet Italian sausage in this recipe.*

chili mac

prep 15 minutes I **cook** 30 minutes I **makes** 4 servings

1 pound ground beef
1 cup Pace® Picante Sauce
1 tablespoon chili powder
1 can (14.5 ounces) whole peeled tomatoes, drained and
    cut up
1 cup frozen whole kernel corn
1½ cups elbow macaroni, cooked and drained (about 3 cups)
½ cup shredded Cheddar cheese
    Sliced avocado **and** sour cream

1. Cook the beef in a 10-inch skillet over medium-high heat until it's well browned, stirring often to separate the meat. Pour off any fat.

2. Stir the picante sauce, chili powder, tomatoes and corn in the skillet and heat to a boil. Reduce the heat to low. Cook for 10 minutes.

3. Stir in the macaroni. Top with the cheese. Cover and cook until the cheese is melted. Garnish with the avocado and sour cream.

country chicken stew

prep 15 minutes | **cook** 40 minutes | **makes** 4 servings

- 2 slices bacon, diced
- 1 medium onion, sliced (about ½ cup)
- 1 can (10¾ ounces) Campbell's® Condensed Cream of Chicken Soup (Regular *or* 98% Fat Free)
- 1 soup can water
- ½ teaspoon dried oregano leaves, crushed
- 3 medium potatoes, cut into 1-inch pieces (about 3 cups)
- 2 medium carrots, sliced (about 1 cup)
- 1 cup frozen cut green beans
- 2 cans (4.5 ounces *each*) Swanson® Premium White Chunk Chicken Breast in Water, drained
- 2 tablespoons chopped fresh parsley

1. Cook the bacon in a 10-inch skillet over medium-high heat until crisp, stirring often. Remove the bacon from the skillet and drain on paper towels.

2. Add the onion to the skillet and cook until tender, stirring occasionally. Stir in the soup, water, oregano, potatoes and carrots and heat to a boil. Reduce the heat to low. Cover and cook for 15 minutes.

3. Stir the beans in the skillet. Cover and cook for 10 minutes or until the vegetables are tender. Stir in the chicken, parsley and bacon and cook until the mixture is hot and bubbling.

tip Substitute *1 can* (8 ounces) cut green beans, drained, for the frozen. Add the green beans with the chicken.

chicken sorrento

prep 20 minutes **I cook** 20 minutes **I makes** 4 servings

- 1 tablespoon vegetable oil
- 1 pound skinless, boneless chicken breast halves
- 1 jar (24 ounces) Prego® Veggie Smart® Chunky & Savory Italian Sauce
- 2 tablespoons balsamic vinegar
- 2 tablespoons chopped fresh basil leaves
- 3 cups penne pasta, cooked and drained (about 4½ cups)
- ¼ cup grated Parmesan cheese

1. Heat the oil in a 10-inch skillet over medium-high heat. Add the chicken and cook for 10 minutes or until well browned on both sides. Remove the chicken from the skillet.

2. Stir the Italian sauce and vinegar in the skillet and cook for 2 minutes, stirring often. Stir in the basil. Return the chicken to the skillet. Reduce the heat to low. Cover and cook for 5 minutes or until the chicken is cooked through.

3. Slice the chicken. Serve the chicken and sauce over the penne. Sprinkle with the cheese.

mexican pizza

thaw 40 minutes I **prep** 20 minutes I **bake** 15 minutes
makes 4 servings

- ½ of a 17.3-ounce package Pepperidge Farm® Puff Pastry Sheets (1 sheet), thawed
- ¾ cup Prego® Traditional Italian Sauce
- ¼ cup Pace® Picante Sauce
- ¾ cup shredded mozzarella cheese
- ¾ cup shredded Cheddar cheese
- ¼ cup sliced pitted ripe olives

1. Heat the oven to 400°F.

2. Unfold the pastry sheet on a lightly floured surface. Roll the pastry sheet into a 15×10-inch rectangle. Place the pastry onto a baking sheet. Prick the pastry thoroughly with a fork. Bake for 10 minutes or until the pastry is golden brown.

3. Stir the Italian sauce and picante sauce in a small bowl. Spread the sauce mixture on the pastry to within ½ inch of the edge. Top with the cheeses and sprinkle with the olives. Bake for 5 minutes or until the cheese is melted.

chicken cacciatore & pasta skillet

prep 10 minutes | **cook** 30 minutes | **makes** 4 servings

- 1 tablespoon vegetable oil
- 1¼ pounds skinless, boneless chicken breast halves **or** skinless, boneless chicken thighs
- 1¾ cups Swanson® Chicken Broth **or** Swanson® Chicken Stock
- 1 teaspoon dried oregano leaves, crushed
- 1 teaspoon garlic powder
- 1 can (14.5 ounces) diced tomatoes
- 1 small green pepper, cut into 2-inch-long strips (about 1 cup)
- 1 medium onion, cut into wedges
- ¼ teaspoon ground black pepper
- ½ of a 1-pound package **uncooked** medium shell-shaped pasta (about 2½ cups)

1. Heat the oil in a 10-inch skillet over medium-high heat. Add the chicken and cook for 10 minutes or until well browned on both sides.

2. Stir the broth, oregano, garlic powder, tomatoes, green pepper, onion and black pepper in the skillet and heat to a boil. Stir in the pasta. Reduce the heat to low. Cover and cook for 15 minutes or until the pasta is tender.

asian chicken with peanuts

prep 15 minutes I **cook** 20 minutes I **makes** 4 servings

- 2 tablespoons cornstarch
- 1¾ cups Swanson® Chicken Stock
- 2 tablespoons soy sauce
- ½ teaspoon ground ginger
- ½ teaspoon sesame oil (optional)
- 2 tablespoons vegetable oil
- 1 pound skinless, boneless chicken breasts, cut into strips
- 2 cups broccoli florets
- 2 small red peppers, cut into 2-inch-long strips (about 2 cups)
- 2 cloves garlic, minced
- ½ cup salted peanuts

  Hot cooked regular long-grain white rice

1. Stir the cornstarch, stock, soy sauce, ginger and sesame oil, if desired, in a medium bowl until the mixture is smooth.

2. Heat **1 tablespoon** of the oil in a 12-inch skillet over medium-high heat. Add the chicken and stir-fry until well browned, stirring often. Remove the chicken from the skillet.

3. Reduce the heat to medium. Heat the remaining vegetable oil in the skillet. Add the broccoli, peppers and garlic and stir-fry until the vegetables are tender-crisp. Stir the cornstarch mixture in the skillet.

Cook and stir until the mixture boils and thickens. Return the chicken to the skillet. Stir in the peanuts and cook until the mixture is hot and bubbling. Serve over the rice.

2-step inside-out chicken pot pie

prep 10 minutes I **cook** 15 minutes I **makes** 4 servings

- 4 skinless, boneless chicken breast halves (about 1 pound), cut into 1-inch pieces
- 1 can (10¾ ounces) Campbell's® Condensed Cream of Chicken Soup (Regular *or* 98% Fat Free)
- 1 bag (16 ounces) frozen vegetable combination (broccoli, cauliflower, carrots)
- 8 hot biscuits, split

1. Cook the chicken in a 10-inch nonstick skillet over medium-high heat until well browned, stirring often.

2. Stir the soup and vegetables in the skillet. Reduce the heat to low. Cover and cook until the chicken is cooked through. Serve the chicken and sauce over the biscuits.

25-minute chicken & noodles

prep 5 minutes | **cook** 20 minutes | **makes** 4 servings

1¾ cups Swanson® Chicken Stock

1 teaspoon dried basil leaves, crushed

¼ teaspoon ground black pepper

2 cups frozen vegetable combination (broccoli, cauliflower, carrots)

2 cups *uncooked* medium egg noodles

2 cups cubed cooked chicken

1. Heat the stock, basil, black pepper and vegetables in a 10-inch skillet over medium heat to a boil. Reduce the heat to low. Cover and cook for 5 minutes or until the vegetables are tender-crisp.

2. Stir the noodles in the skillet. Cover and cook for 5 minutes or until the noodles are tender. Stir in the chicken and cook until the mixture is hot and bubbling.

garlic chicken, vegetable & rice skillet

prep 5 minutes **I** **cook** 40 minutes **I** **makes** 4 servings

    Vegetable cooking spray
1¼ pounds skinless, boneless chicken breast halves
2 cloves garlic, minced
1¾ cups Swanson® Chicken Stock
¾ cup *uncooked* regular long-grain white rice
1 bag (16 ounces) frozen vegetable combination
      (broccoli, cauliflower, carrots)
⅓ cup grated Parmesan cheese
    Paprika

1. Spray a 12-inch skillet with the cooking spray and heat over medium-high heat for 1 minute. Add the chicken and garlic and cook for 10 minutes or until the chicken is well browned on both sides. Remove the chicken from the skillet.

2. Stir the stock, rice and vegetables in the skillet and heat to a boil. Reduce the heat to low. Cover and cook for 15 minutes. Stir in the cheese.

3. Return the chicken to the skillet. Sprinkle the chicken with the paprika. Cover and cook for 10 minutes or until the chicken is cooked through and the rice is tender.

easy turkey & biscuits

prep 20 minutes | **bake** 30 minutes | **makes** 5 servings

- 1 can (10¾ ounces) Campbell's® Condensed Cream of Celery Soup (Regular *or* 98% Fat Free)
- 1 can (10¾ ounces) Campbell's® Condensed Cream of Potato Soup
- 1 cup milk
- ¼ teaspoon dried thyme leaves, crushed
- ¼ teaspoon ground black pepper
- 4 cups cooked cut-up vegetables (broccoli, cauliflower, carrots)
- 2 cups cubed cooked turkey *or* cooked chicken
- 1 package refrigerated buttermilk biscuits (10 biscuits)

1. Stir the soups, milk, thyme, black pepper, vegetables and turkey in a 3-quart shallow baking dish.

2. Bake at 400°F. for 15 minutes. Stir the turkey mixture. Cut **each** biscuit into quarters.

3. Evenly top the turkey mixture with the cut biscuits. Bake for 15 minutes or until the turkey mixture is hot and bubbling and the biscuits are golden brown.

tip *To microwave the vegetables, stir the vegetables in a 2-quart shallow microwave-safe baking dish with ¼ **cup** water. Cover and microwave on HIGH for 10 minutes.*

monterey chicken tortilla casserole

prep 15 minutes I **bake** 40 minutes I **makes** 4 servings

- 1 **cup coarsely crumbled tortilla chips**
- 2 **cups cubed cooked chicken *or* turkey**
- 1 **can (about 15 ounces) cream-style corn**
- ¾ **cup Pace® Picante Sauce**
- ½ **cup sliced pitted ripe olives**
- 2 **ounces shredded Cheddar cheese (about ½ cup)**
   Chopped green *or* red pepper
   Tortilla chips

1. Layer the crumbled chips, chicken, corn and picante sauce in a 1-quart casserole. Top with the olives and cheese.

2. Bake at 350°F. for 40 minutes or until the mixture is hot and bubbling. Top with the pepper. Serve with the chips.

mexican chicken & rice

prep 10 minutes I **cook** 30 minutes I **makes** 5 servings

- 1¾ cups Swanson® Chicken Stock
- ½ teaspoon ground cumin
- ⅛ teaspoon ground black pepper
- 1 medium onion, chopped (about ½ cup)
- 1 small green pepper, chopped (about ½ cup)
- ¾ cup *uncooked* regular long-grain white rice
- 1 can (about 15 ounces) kidney beans, rinsed and drained
- 2 cans (4.5 ounces *each*) Swanson® Premium White Chunk Chicken Breast in Water, drained

1. Heat the stock, cumin, black pepper, onion and green pepper in a 3-quart saucepan over medium heat to a boil.

2. Stir the rice in the saucepan. Reduce the heat to low. Cover and cook for 20 minutes or until the rice is tender.

3. Stir in the beans and chicken and cook until the mixture is heated through.

simple creamy chicken risotto

prep 10 minutes | **cook** 35 minutes | **makes** 4 servings

- 1 tablespoon vegetable oil
- 4 skinless, boneless chicken breast halves (about 1 pound), cut into 1-inch pieces
- 1 can (10¾ ounces) Campbell's® Condensed Cream of Mushroom with Roasted Garlic Soup
- 1 can (10½ ounces) Campbell's® Condensed Chicken Broth
- ¾ cup water
- 1 small carrot, shredded (about ¼ cup)
- 2 green onions, sliced (about ¼ cup)
- 1 tablespoon grated Parmesan cheese
- 1 cup *uncooked* regular long-grain white rice

1. Heat the oil in a 10-inch skillet over medium-high heat. Add the chicken and cook until well browned, stirring often.

2. Stir the soup, broth, water, carrot, green onions and cheese in the skillet and heat to a boil. Stir in the rice. Reduce the heat to low. Cover and cook for 25 minutes or until the chicken is cooked through and the rice is tender.

pork chops & french onion rice

prep 10 minutes I **cook** 30 minutes I **makes** 6 servings

- 1 tablespoon vegetable oil
- 6 bone-in pork chops (about 2 pounds)
- 1 can (10½ ounces) Campbell's® Condensed French Onion Soup
- ½ cup water
  Ground black pepper
- 1 stalk celery, chopped (about ½ cup)
- ¼ teaspoon dried thyme leaves, crushed
- ½ cup *uncooked* regular long-grain white rice

1. Heat the oil in a 10-inch skillet over medium-high heat. Add the pork and cook until well browned on both sides. Pour off any fat.

2. Stir the soup, water, black pepper, celery, thyme and rice in the skillet and heat to a boil. Reduce the heat to low. Cover and cook for 30 minutes or until the pork is cooked through and the rice is tender, stirring the rice occasionally.

picante chicken & rice bake

prep 10 minutes | **cook** 45 minutes | **makes** 4 servings

1   jar (16 ounces) Pace® Picante Sauce
½ cup water
1   cup whole kernel corn
¾ cup *uncooked* regular long-grain white rice
4   skinless, boneless chicken breast halves (about 1 pound)
     Paprika
½ cup shredded Cheddar cheese

1. Stir the picante sauce, water, corn and rice in a 2-quart shallow baking dish. Top with the chicken. Sprinkle the chicken with the paprika. **Cover** the baking dish.

2. Bake at 375°F. for 45 minutes or until the chicken is cooked through and the rice is tender. Sprinkle with the cheese.

tip *If you don't have Cheddar cheese on hand, you can substitute an equal amount of shredded Monterey Jack **or** a Mexican cheese blend.*

penne bolognese–style

prep 20 minutes | **cook** 30 minutes | **makes** 4 servings

- 1 pound lean ground beef
- 1 large onion, minced (about 1 cup)
- 3 large carrots, shredded (about 2 cups)
- 1 jar (24 ounces) Prego® Veggie Smart® Smooth & Simple Italian Sauce
- ½ cup water
- 3 tablespoons fresh basil leaves, cut into very thin strips
- 3 cups penne pasta, cooked and drained (about 4½ cups)
- 2 tablespoons grated Parmesan cheese

1. Cook the beef, onion and carrots in a 12-inch skillet over medium-high heat until the beef is well browned, stirring often to separate the meat. Pour off any fat.

2. Stir the Italian sauce and water in the skillet and heat to a boil. Reduce the heat to low. Cook for 15 minutes or until the vegetables are tender, stirring occasionally. Stir in additional water, if needed, until desired consistency.

3. Place the basil and penne into a large bowl. Add the beef mixture and toss to coat. Sprinkle with the cheese.

quick chicken a la king

prep 20 minutes **I** **cook** 10 minutes **I** **makes** 4 servings

- 1 tablespoon butter
- ¼ cup chopped green pepper **or** red pepper
- 1 can (10¾ ounces) Campbell's® Condensed Cream of Mushroom Soup (Regular **or** 98% Fat Free)
- ½ cup milk
- 1½ cups cubed cooked chicken **or** ham
- 4 cups hot cooked regular long-grain white rice

1. Heat the butter in a 3-quart saucepan over medium heat. Add the pepper and cook until tender, stirring often.

2. Stir the soup, milk and chicken in the skillet and cook until the mixture is hot and bubbling. Serve the chicken mixture with the rice.

classic tuna noodle casserole

prep 10 minutes | **bake** 25 minutes | **makes** 4 servings

1 can (10¾ ounces) Campbell's® Condensed Cream of
  Celery Soup (Regular *or* 98% Fat Free)

½ cup milk

1 cup cooked peas

2 tablespoons chopped pimientos

2 cans (about 6 ounces *each*) tuna, drained and flaked

2 cups hot cooked medium egg noodles

2 tablespoons dry bread crumbs

1 tablespoon butter, melted

1. Heat the oven to 400°F. Stir the soup, milk, peas, pimientos, tuna
and noodles in a 1½-quart baking dish. Stir the bread crumbs and
butter in a small bowl.

2. Bake for 20 minutes or until the tuna mixture is hot and bubbling.
Stir the tuna mixture. Sprinkle with the bread crumb mixture.

3. Bake for 5 minutes or until the bread crumbs are golden brown.

tip *Substitute Campbell's® Condensed Cream of Mushroom Soup*
for the Cream
of Celery. To
melt the butter,
remove the
wrapper and
place the butter
in a microwavable
cup. Cover and
microwave
on HIGH for
30 seconds.

green bean casserole

prep 10 minutes I **bake** 30 minutes I **makes** 5 servings

> 1   can (10¾ ounces) Campbell's® Condensed Cream of
>   Mushroom Soup (Regular *or* 98% Fat Free)
> ½   cup milk
> 1   teaspoon soy sauce
>   Dash ground black pepper
> 2   packages (10 ounces *each*) frozen cut green beans,
>   cooked and drained
> 1   can (2.8 ounces) French fried onions (1⅓ cups)

1. Stir the soup, milk, soy sauce, black pepper, green beans and
⅔ **cup** onions in a 1½-quart casserole.

2. Bake at 350°F. for 25 minutes or until hot. Stir the green bean
mixture.

3. Sprinkle the remaining onions over the green bean mixture. Bake
for 5 minutes more or until onions are golden brown.

tip *You can also make this classic side dish with fresh **or** canned
green beans. You will need either 1½ **pounds** fresh green beans,
cut into 1-inch
pieces, cooked
and drained **or**
2 cans (about
16 ounces
each) cut
green beans,
drained for the
frozen green
beans.*

2-bean chili

prep 10 minutes I **cook** 15 minutes I **makes** 6 servings

- 1 pound ground beef
- 1 large green pepper, chopped (about 1 cup)
- 1 large onion, chopped (about 1 cup)
- 2 tablespoons chili powder
- ¼ teaspoon ground black pepper
- 3 cups Campbell's® Tomato Juice
- 1 can (about 15 ounces) kidney beans, rinsed and drained
- 1 can (about 15 ounces) great Northern beans, rinsed and drained

  Sour cream

  Sliced green onions

  Shredded Cheddar cheese

  Chopped tomato

1. Cook the beef, green pepper, onion, chili powder and black pepper in a 10-inch skillet until the beef is well browned, stirring often to separate the meat. Pour off any fat.

2. Stir the tomato juice and beans in the skillet and cook until the mixture is hot and bubbling. Top the beef mixture with the sour cream, green onions, cheese and tomato before serving.

ranchero enchilada casserole

prep 10 minutes I **bake** 25 minutes I **makes** 4 servings

- 1 can (10¾ ounces) Campbell's® Condensed Cream of Chicken Soup (Regular **or** 98% Fat Free)
- ½ cup water
- 1 teaspoon chili powder
- ½ teaspoon garlic powder
- 1 can (about 4 ounces) chopped green chiles
- ¼ cup rinsed, drained canned black beans
- 3 tablespoons tomato paste
- 2 tablespoons chopped red peppers
- 2 cups cubed cooked chicken
- 4 flour tortillas (8-inch) **or** 6 corn tortillas (6-inch), cut into strips
- ½ cup shredded Cheddar cheese

1. Stir the soup, water, chili powder, garlic powder, chiles, beans, tomato paste, red pepper, chicken and tortillas in a large bowl.

2. Spoon the chicken mixture into a 2-quart shallow baking dish. Top with the cheese. Cover the baking dish.

3. Bake at 350°F. for 25 minutes or until the mixture is hot and bubbling.

country chicken casserole

prep 10 minutes | **bake** 25 minutes | **makes** 5 servings

1 can (10¾ ounces) Campbell's® Condensed Cream of Celery Soup (Regular **or** 98% Fat Free)

1 can (10¾ ounces) Campbell's® Condensed Cream of Potato Soup

1 cup milk

¼ teaspoon dried thyme leaves, crushed

⅛ teaspoon ground black pepper

4 cups cooked cut-up vegetables*

2 cups cubed cooked chicken **or** turkey

4 cups prepared Pepperidge Farm® Herb Seasoned Stuffing

Use a combination of cut green beans and sliced carrots.

1. Stir the soups, milk, thyme, black pepper, vegetables and chicken in a 3-quart shallow baking dish. Top with the stuffing.

2. Bake at 400°F. for 25 minutes or until the stuffing is golden brown.

lightened up beef & vegetable stir-fry

prep 25 minutes **I cook** 25 minutes **I makes** 4 servings

Vegetable cooking spray

1 pound boneless beef sirloin steak, ¾-inch thick (about 1 pound), sliced into very thin strips

2 cups broccoli florets

6 ounces sliced mushrooms (about 2 cups)

2 medium onions, cut into wedges

½ teaspoon garlic powder *or* 2 cloves garlic, minced

1 can (10¾ ounces) Campbell's® Healthy Request® Condensed Cream of Mushroom Soup

½ cup water

1 tablespoon low-sodium soy sauce

1 cup regular long-grain white rice, cooked according to package directions without salt (about 3 cups)

1. Spray a 12-inch skillet with the cooking spray and heat over medium-high heat for 1 minute. Add the beef and cook until well browned, stirring often. Remove the beef from the skillet and set aside.

2. Remove the skillet from the heat and spray with the cooking spray. Add the broccoli, mushrooms, onions and garlic powder and cook until the vegetables are tender-crisp, stirring often.

3. Stir the soup, water and soy sauce in the skillet and heat to a boil. Return the beef to the skillet and cook until cooked through. Serve the beef mixture over the rice.

tip *To make slicing easier, freeze beef for 1 hour.*

chili & rice

prep 10 minutes I **cook** 25 minutes I **makes** 4 servings

¾ **pound ground beef (85% lean)**

1 **medium onion, chopped (about ½ cup)**

1 **tablespoon chili powder**

1 **can (10¾ ounces) Campbell's® Healthy Request®
   Condensed Tomato Soup**

¼ **cup water**

1 **teaspoon vinegar**

1 **can (about 15 ounces) kidney beans, rinsed and drained**

4 **cups hot cooked regular long-grain white rice, cooked
   without salt**

1. Cook the beef, onion and chili powder in a 10-inch skillet over medium-high heat until the beef is well browned, stirring often. Pour off any fat.

2. Stir the soup, water, vinegar and beans in the skillet and heat to a boil. Reduce the heat to low. Cook for 10 minutes or until the mixture is hot and bubbling. Serve the beef mixture over the rice.

tip *This dish is delicious served topped with shredded reduced-fat Cheddar cheese.*

skillet cheesy chicken & rice

prep 5 minutes | **cook** 35 minutes | **makes** 4 servings

- 1 **tablespoon vegetable oil**
- 1¼ **pounds skinless, boneless chicken breast halves**
- 1 **can (10¾ ounces) Campbell's® Condensed Cream of Chicken Soup (Regular *or* 98% Fat Free)**
- 1½ **cups water**
- ½ **teaspoon onion powder**
- ¼ **teaspoon ground black pepper**
- 1 **cup *uncooked* regular long-grain white rice**
- 2 **cups frozen mixed vegetables**
- ½ **cup shredded Cheddar cheese**

1. Heat the oil in a 12-inch skillet over medium-high heat. Add the chicken and cook for 10 minutes or until well browned on both sides. Remove the chicken from the skillet.

2. Stir the soup, water, onion powder, black pepper and rice in the skillet and heat to a boil. Reduce the heat to low. Cover and cook for 15 minutes, stirring once halfway through the cooking time.

3. Stir in the vegetables. Return the chicken to the skillet. Sprinkle with the cheese. Cover and cook for 5 minutes or until the chicken is cooked through and the rice is tender.